CALIFORNIA SOUTHERN
writing from the road, 1992-2025

Adolfo Guzman-Lopez

CALIFORNIA SOUTHERN
writing from the road, 1992-2025

POETRY

Guzman-Lopez, Adolfo

California Southern: writing from the road, 1992-2025. / by Adolfo
Guzman-Lopez.–First edition.

p.158 ; 8.5" x 5.5"

ISBN 978-1-954640-07-8

1. Poetry–21st Century. 2. Latinx poetry–California. 3. Identity and
culture–Poetry. 4. Los Angeles–Poetry.

PS3558.E74 C57 2025

2025933578

Published by HINCHA Press
Edited by *Yago Cura*
Designed by *Svitlana Matus*
First edition ISBN print: 978-1-954640-07-8

Contents

OTHER PROJECTS

Eternal gratitude

Some of the writing in this book has appeared in the following publications:

Beyond Baroque Magazine Vol. 26 No. 2 "We My Love"

Santa Monica Review Fall 2021 "Boom Town National City"

City Works 2008 "Salvador" "The New San Diego"

The National City Public Library "On the Opening of the New National City Public Library"

Geography of Rage: Remembering the Los Angeles Riots of 1992 "The Capital of Aztlan Burns"

Esopus "Ray Say Ta"

The Taco Shop Poets Anthology "A Taco Shop Canto for War-Town San Diego" "Nooks"

LocavorelitLA/Light Bringer Project "Vine A Los Angeles"

Voz/Multimedia Militia "The Movement"

I would also like to thank Lysa, Jordan, Elyanna and all my families in Mexico and the U.S., including my teachers and the Temple Israel Long Beach community.

Acknowledgement to the poets and writers from Mexico, the U.S., and other countries who I've collaborated with over the years. The taco shop poetry crews from 1994 to 2004. The Spine of Califas poetry, performance crews, especially Xiuy Velo and Willie Herron. People I admire: Dolores Dorantes, Maria Figueroa, Michelle Téllez, Tim Z. Hernandez, Yago S. Cura, María Elena Fernández, Mike Sonksen, Imani Tolliver, William Archila, Darren J. de Leon, Rojo Cordova, George Kalmar and everyone in the Project 1521 crew.

The L.A. homies: Omar, George, Elon, Anna, Sara (Radiosonideros!), Ruben Martinez and Ruben Guevara, and all the Chicane, Chicanx, Chicana, Chicano camaradas over the years.

The KPBS crews from 1995-2000, in particular the production team for The Lounge. The KPCC/LAist crews from 2000-2025, especially the Forgotten Revolutionary crew at LAist Studios, the folks at Participant Media who championed the podcast. Cheryl Devall and all the good editors I've had over the years. The magazine, newspaper, and public radio editors who have said yes to my story pitches. Juan Devis. The CSU Long Beach faculty who have helped me teach Journalism 382.

And what would I be without all the knowledge, generosity, and so much more shared by all the people who have said yes when I've asked them for an interview for a news story.

Thank you.

Towards peace/paz/Shalom

Introduction

In *California Southern*, Adolfo Guzman-Lopez venerates the sacred altars of his experience. Beginning in San Diego in 1994 as a founding member of the influential Taco Shop Poets, Guzman-Lopez's investigative poetry eventually brought him to Los Angeles where he became an award-winning reporter for KPCC/LAist, the NPR affiliate. These poems "capture the leaving of your home, the wind through the window, the dust from the fields and roads, and seeing wary eyes and friendly smiles at our destinations" while revering cultural, historical and personal landscapes from Baja to San Francisco.

"Fill your fountain pen with blood, fill it with the rainbow ink sliding down the corner of your eye. Write your own postcard," effuses Guzman-Lopez in the prose poem, "Boom Town National City." *California Southern* collects the poet's blood-soaked postcards through his rite of passage. Born in Mexico City then moving to Tijuana when he was three then settling in National City at seven, our poet then spent the next 17 years in this suburban enclave located in the South Bay section of San Diego County.

National City is just west of Mt. San Miguel, the highest point within the San Diego Metro area. National City's undulating topography is a major factor in why it is a city with binaries: a Heights, a barrio, a movie palace, an amphitheater, a boulevard for low riders, mansions on the hill, lush little league fields. National City for Guzman-Lopez is "where the scrap metal yards form a mountain of blessings and a mountain of curses. It's where a studio apartment on McKinley, in Old Town National City, led to three homes for my mother and stepfather."

His mother and stepfather worked multiple jobs as they slowly but surely manifested their California dream. "My mother," he writes, "cleaned five houses in the same neighborhood so my Pacific Beach school uniform was Op (Ocean Pacific) cord shorts and a Lightning Bolt shirt. My chariot was a fiberglass G&S skateboard with knobby orange wheels that played a different 33 ⅓ melody on the sandy Mission Beach boardwalk Monday through Friday."

Like the double consciousness of W.E.B. DuBois, Guzman-Lopez walked in the duplicitous San Diego world between his mother's nonstop work schedule and the Op cord shorts he rocked on the Mission Beach boardwalk. "I learned to be a Chicano," he says, "while living in and leaving National City."

"Boom Town National City," is pivotal because it mediates the concrete specifics of daily life and otherworldly cosmology that come together in this book. The juxtaposition of Mt. San Miguel against the city's humble streets creates a focal point, making the mountain a mythical beacon of promise looming over the city. "So much silt brought from the mountains' inner thighs it makes the bay shallow enough for you to walk on," he states. "You can walk on water in National City. But lose faith in yourself and you sink. Hold on long enough and you'll reach the other side."

Arriving at UC San Diego in the late 1980s, Guzman-Lopez had an inherent understanding of California cities with "19th century and 20th century post-war middle-class grids." In college he became politically active, writing poems, attending punk shows and exploring every San Diego corner. By 1993 he recited poetry at Cafe Chabalaba in the still rough around the edges downtown. A small, independent coffee shop with a Stevie Ray Vaughan mural on the outside wall. He recalls the cafe's "dusty couches, hand painted chairs, tables, walls."

In August of 1994, while working at San Diego's Centro Cultural de la Raza, he started a month-long reading series that went on for over a year. "It coalesced," he recalls "into me, Adrian Arancibia, Miguel Angel Soria, Tomas Riley, Kevin Green on drums and Mikey Figgins on bass." They called themselves "The Taco Shop Poets," because they "wanted to affirm taco shops as spaces with their own cultural spirit (the music of the jukeboxes, the literature of the freebie newspapers) and sought to meld spoken word with the patrons of those spaces."

With poems like "A Taco Shop Canto for War-Town San Diego," Guzman-Lopez's timing was kismet. Spoken word poetry's electricity melted perfectly with the 90s punk, hip hop and grunge ethos. Simultaneously, the Taco Shop Poets embodied San Diego's bilingual border culture. The stars aligned synchronously as Adolfo and the Taco Shop Poets epitomized the moment: "Now navy-town grunge / oozes from sidewalk cracks / onto marble floored lobbies / grabbing tourists by their ankles / dragging them / into the ground waters of free speech."

The Taco Shop Poets toured California, being especially active in Downtown San Diego at the Centro Cultural de la Raza and El Campo Ruse where they performed from 1994 to 1999. These independent, underground art spaces featured "hand made, hand run, experimental music, poetry, performance by people of all races and ethnicities." The Taco Shop Poets were so prolific that they were even joined by the Chicano poetry legend, Alurista for about a year in 1995. By the late 90s, the collective gradually dissolved as the poets went their separate ways, got married, and transitioned into their careers. Guzman-Lopez never stopped writing poems.

In October of 2000, Guzman-Lopez moved to Los Angeles to become a reporter at Southern California Public Radio, the NPR affiliate. The interrogative spirit of his writing made him perfect for the airwaves where he recorded audio stories and wrote online articles. Concurrently he wrote poems like "Vine a Los Angeles." "The eagle / perched on the cactus / called me to Los Angeles," he declares, reminding us that "the frogs / sleep under the concrete, / the rows of grape vines / sleep under the concrete." As the poem concludes he urges readers to "use your hands, / dig deep. / Use your nose, / dig deep. / Use your mouth, / dig deep. / Use your heart, / dig deep."

California Southern digs deep into the Golden State's past in pieces like "The Capital of Aztlan Burns." There's a litany of images: "Palmeras brought for 1932 Olympics / sunglasses melt / palm trees burn / Sol, arena, sangre / seeping out of the streets / of fantastic Losangelestitlan." The poet's Spanglish compounds the verisimilitude and rhythm of his vision.

Embedded in these poems are questions but if you keep reading there are answers. Take "Spine of Califas - Morning Crossing." "What are you bringing?," he asks. "A fractured identity, / milquetoast bilingualism, / resentment of how you treat my hermanos, / a desire to unzip the border, / a dream that the wall dissolves / and turns into water that reaches / the dormant lavender roots / that'll grow 15-feet tall." Adolfo sees that another world is possible for those who want it.

California Southern emerges from a lineage that includes Octavio Paz, Carlos Fuentes, Jack Kerouac, Gregory Corso, the bilingual poetry of Alurista, Oscar Zeta Acosta and Adolfo's Tijuana aunts who were educators and his early mentors. He also holds a special place in his heart for the Nuyorican transplant poet Jesus "Papoleto" Melendez who he saw perform in 1993 while working at the Centro Cultural de la Raza. Melendez blew him away, performing bilingual poems with a keyboardist and acoustic bass. "Papoleto rocked my world," he says, "made me say, I want to do that." Within a few months Adolfo jammed poetry all over San Diego.

Three decades later, Adolfo Guzman-Lopez's hundreds of poems embody a prolific oeuvre of work. *California Southern* maps "la linea, where X marks the spot, where the Spine of Califas begins. / Where the vendors are unionized, / where the vendors sell plaster hamburgers, / where the vendors sell surfing chimps, / where the vendors sell velvet paintings of John Wayne, Trump with a bullseye, / Duchamp, Dolores Huerta, Marcos, Kissinger, Don Francisco, Mendieta, and Anzaldúa." These poetic cantos are cultural, historical and personal while honoring the ancestors, forecasting the future and meditating on sacred altars of experience.

Mike Sonksen
Poet, journalist, LA historian,
Author of *Letters to My City*

Foreword

Adolfo Guzman-Lopez's *California Southern* is a memoir disguised as a road trip guide-book from the Tijuana-Mexican border to Los Angeles and central Cali, disguised as a book of poems. While its progression is marked geographically, beware this is no exhilarating joy ride through new territories of pleasure for the carefree tourist. Instead it's a profound and moving memoir of a little boy from Mexico City turned Tijuana transplant, transplanted again to el otro lado, National City and San Diego, surviving the not-so-fun house mirrors of class and race on the educational path into the U.S. middle class, then finally a chosen re-planting to Los Angeles to grow his career as a journalist. *California Southern* is an immigrant story, a Chicane border story and a love letter to his adopted city, Los Angeles. A road trip, yes, and a trip.

Guzman-Lopez is a master documenter of place, honed, no doubt, by his lifelong oficio as a reporter, for over two decades now with NPR affiliate LAist 89.3fm. So one of the gifts of this volume is that la linea-the border line in Tijuana to cross into the U.S., National City, San Diego and Los Angeles are all major characters. Vulnerability is *California Southern*'s second gift, shining most splendorous in the excavation of the tumult and alienation of navigating shame, rage and seductions of assimilation with a nopal en la frente on the road to a border Chicane identity. These revelations are Guzman-Lopez's lived experience to Gloria Anzaldua's borderland theory of "la herida abierta . . . the open wound where the first world grates against the third and bleeds . . . splits me splits me/ me raja me raja" (*Borderlands/La Frontera*) This chronological and geographical border story, draws elements from paths carved by Guzman-Lopez's Califas Chicano border literary elders: Alurista, Juan Felipe Herrera and Luis Alberto Urrea, also shaped by their lives on the Tijuana-San Diego border.

Guzman-Lopez brings his reporter's eye and a poet's pen to scenes of the border, San Diego and LA neighborhoods. In "Morning Crossing" he captures the TJ/SD border crossing scene, "Car exhaust mixes with sweat evaporating on the foreheads of: / the newspaper vendors, / the plaster monkey vendors, / the plaster cactus vendors, / the plaster Uncle Sam vendors, / the plaster Sleeping Mexican vendors . . ." Wielding, as he frequently does, his deft hand at repetition, he nails the scene that so many times I witnessed crossing back to L.A. from Tijuana growing up, whenever my Mexico City immigrant parents missed their homeland. But Guzman-Lopez reminds us this is not just a weekend jaunt for tourists or nostalgic Mexican immigrants, it's daily life for him and many: las señoras, the college student going to her swap meet job, the mom taking her son to Catholic school.

The border is where Guzman-Lopez's vulnerability makes you catch your breath, a magnet embedded in his lyrics of the losses and complexities of a childhood of border living and border crossing. In "Al Norte," again at the border crossing heading north, there is a brilliantly structured section with all the questions we're asked by border patrol: "Where were you born? . . Where are you going? . . . What are you bringing? / A fractured identity, / milquetoast bilingualism," Then utters all of our seething yet unspoken quintessential Chicane response: "Resentment of how you treat my hermanos." It's that same rage and indignation that fuels his border poet elder, legendary Chicano poet and former US poet laureate Juan Felipe Herrera's book, *Everyday We Get More Illegal*, the rage of Chicane consciousness.

His vulnerability takes its deepest dive in another pair of poems reflecting Guzman-Lopez's double life of class and race hierarchies he kickflips in and out of on the U.S. side in San Diego. *PBJH*, a deceptively innocuous title for this short prose poem that drops a bomb (a frequent strategy) reveals his undocumented-son-of-a-housekeeper status yet immersed in the social class of his mom's white middle-class employers because he's classmates with their kids. So Op (Ocean Pacific) corduroy shorts, signifier of (blond) California surfer identity, become his longed for prenda of belonging, he already had a skateboard. Legal acceptance en el otro lado comes with the 1986 Amnesty law at the end of high school.

"Wrestle" feels like Guzman-Lopez's signature declaration of surviving the border chingazos of identity at different stages of his youth. It's an all-out wrestling match to make and claim internal space, the tumbling turmoil to find a place within himself for his bilingual bicultural whole self. It's Guzman-Lopez's elaboration on the dilemma with which Corky Gonzalez opens, "I Am Joaquin" his seminal 1967 Chicano identity-defining poem "I am Joaquin, lost in a world of confusion/caught up in the whirl of a gringo society . . . / I must choose between the paradox of / victory of the spirit, despite physical hunger, / or to exist in the grasp of American social neurosis." In this battleground, the narrator gains a new name, Salvador, shortened to Sal, that then Guzman-Lopez engages with in playful bilingual word play ("Sal" is the verb to leave or get out in Spanish): "Salgo de dónde / la sal go, / tu sales, / el sale, / nosotros salemos. / Sal si puedes/ Sal va vidas/ Sal si te dan ganas," conveying some kind of maze of confusion, ambivalence, but maybe I better get the hell out. It's a celebration of languages a la Alurista, San Diego Chicano movement poet and guest poet with the Taco Shop Poets for a period, who's code-switching word play is his signature style (*Chicano Duende*). Ultimately the narrator's new name is a disappointment, and reminiscent of Sandra Cisneros' use of protagonist Esperanza's name to reveal the weight of her social and internal worlds in *House on Mango Street*, Guzman-Lopez unravels that Sal's: "only means Struggles with Spanish / Struggles with English / Struggles with absent father / Struggles with fatherless mother /Struggles to remember the final score / Struggles with green, white, and red / Struggles with the red, white, and blue." The heart-breaking longing for a place where all selves and histories are welcomed are conveyed in a single sentence: I want to enter, /next to a sign that says: / DF-TJ-NC-SD-LA-LB-DF-TJ-NC-SD-LA-LB. Yes, me too, Adolfo, me too. This masculine vulnerability rare and most welcome, can also be found forged in Luis Urrea's border identity memoir *Nobody's Son*, that parallels Guzman-Lopez's childhood move from Tijuana to San Diego.

California Southern's other signature strength is its vivid documentation of San Diego and Los Angeles neighborhoods and their cast of characters, much like Sandra Cisneros does for Chicago (*House on Mango Street*) Marisela Norte for East LA (*Peeping Tom Tom Girl*) and Vickie Vértiz for various LA neighborhoods (*Palm Frond With Its Throat Cut*). I didn't know the corner of 5th and Broadway in San Diego. Now I do, after reading the eponymous poem, "Para Trinidad" and "Sal." In this last poem, the corner is peopled by Sal the preacher, the hip-hop pachucos and maids:

> Lives lived out with stubby fingers
> Clorox cracked skin
> And tennis elbow
> From pushing vacuum cleaners
> Sal competes with
> Incense sellers
> Bow tie media moguls
> Making the call
> Homeless selling used bus transfers.

Guzman-Lopez's love letter to LA largely unfolds through many poems about multiple LA neighborHoods. They are poems of loving detail and with each observation the poet seems to grow in intimacy with the city, through its streets and street corners and the noble and not so noble who walk, march and loiter on them, at once giving the reader a sense of the mosaic that is our city. The poem "Evening" doesn't disclose its location, but captures a street corner of Latino immigrant LA, the preacher and church goers in the storefront where "dresses fall beneath the ankle." In contrast, the other corners animated by a street preacher, a homeboy, a señora, obreros, and "a festival of flesh," while a bus rolls by and the homeboy's tattoo seems to be the most sacred of all. Most are portraits of specific neighborhoods, like Westlake and Boyle Heights. The poem "Third and Witmer" paints a portrait of the underage homies in front of the three-story apartment building drinking away the afternoon and in "Evergreen and Brooklyn" the healing hands of the street corner huesera are the focal point.

Most moving is Guzman-Lopez's outright declaration of love to the city in "Neighborhood," a prose poem where Guzman-Lopez brims with love for everyone in LA, "I mean everyone," because his brush with a cop's rubber bullet to the throat while on his reporter's beat in his Long Beach neighborhood, awakened him to the gift of his breath, and all of ours. But it's not platitudes, his point of entry is a list of images of all his encountered neighborhoods because, in a thrilling realization, LA holds all his previous neighborhoods and all LA neighborhoods are his neighborhood. "My LA neighborhood is Peralvillo in Mexico City where I was born, . . . My LA neighborhood is Colonia Aleman, Tijuana where my single mom and I looked over the cliff, at night, to the fields of San Ysidro . . . It's every single corner and sidewalk where I've stood and held my microphone, talking to people en las buenas y en las malas, that's my LA neighborhood."

The collection continues with a few poems driving up "the spine of Califas" into central California and closes cleverly taking the text of the Treaty of Guadalupe into poetic form, "A treaty of peace / Friendship / Limits / And settlement / Between the united states of america /and the united mexican states / Without exception of places or persons." It reads like a longing, a yearning, a dared hope in response to the lacerations of a border childhood, a Chicane life. A reminder that it's in writing, this initial intent. The poet dares to remember, dares to write down again, dares to remind us, however elusive a vision, of what would heal nations and a poet's jagged spine.

María Elena Fernández
Writer, performer, professor
Cal State University Northridge

CALIFORNIA SOUTHERN:

writing from the road, 1992-2025

The Spine of Califas

All you have to do is go back
To when you could barely see out the window
To when you slid across the back seat

Home became the countryside
Home became the open road
Home became the unknown

Remember
How the wind pressed up your palm
How you knew the direction
How the passing of cars became words
How far and near slid at different speeds

That old back seat is covered with dust
And you still put your hand out
You hope the wind holds it

As you drive up the five
As you drive up the 405
As you drive up the 101
As you drive up the 99
As you drive up the Spine of Califas

Morning Crossing

Morning,
north over there.

You're the driver bringing five señoras to work, with tourist visas, $10
round trip.

You're the driver coming back from La Revo, a night of whistles,
tequila,
walking in a dream of neon, bass echoes pulling you into every bar.

You're the mother taking your son to the Catholic school on Riverside
Drive,
you'll breathe easier once he's in medical school.

You're the retired sailor, planted your flag in front of a three bedroom
Tijuana house,
half the rent of a studio apartment in your country.

You're the engineering student crossing to a job at the swap meet.

You're the 25 year-old mexicana, thinking about the money in your
pocket
when you get the car across,
feeling your artery pump double blood,
hands clutched on steering wheel,
                    the back seats firm as a pile of bricks.

You're the political scientist with an ocean view of playas, entertain

La Jolla friends,
each with a cross over dream on the rocks.

You're facing California, your back to Latin America, you want to
stand atop your car and yell:

Papers? Papers? I don't need no stinking papers!

Car exhaust mixes with sweat evaporating on the foreheads of:
the newspaper vendors,
the plaster monkey vendors,
the plaster cactus vendors,
the plaster Uncle Sam vendors,
the plaster Sleeping Mexican vendors.

And out of the corner of your eye, cigarette smoke from a cigarette
holder,
between fingers, in the hills of Tijuana,
where a woman sits on IKEA furniture
and spits on gringos at cocktail parties.

Cars, waves 13 seconds apart, pass layers of wanted posters:
the Pancho Villas, the Arellanos, the Chapos, the Zetas
(the hit men, not the newspaper).

Arteries north,
veins south.

Al Norte

This is la linea, where X marks
the spot, where the Spine of Califas begins.

Where the vendors are unionized,
where the vendors sell plaster hamburgers,
where the vendors sell surfing chimps,
where the vendors sell velvet paintings of John Wayne, Trump with a
bullseye,
Duchamp, Dolores Huerta, Marcos, Kissinger, Don Francisco,
Mendieta, and Anzaldúa.

Nuns ask for donations,
teenagers ask for red cross blood.

Where were you born?
Ni aquí, ni allá,
among the palms,
on a bed of nopales.

Where are you going?
Shopping,
studying,
persisting.

What are you bringing?
A fractured identity,
milquetoast bilingualism,

resentment of how you treat my hermanos,
a desire to unzip the border,
a dream that the wall dissolves
and turns into water that reaches
the dormant lavender roots
that'll grow 15-feet tall.

Nothing to Declare

I was brought to this valley
To see clouds explode over mountains

I was brought to this ocean
To see waves crumble thousand-year old cliffs

I left on Ash Wednesday
Hoping
To find
To lose

The road here
Littered with accents
Sprouting
Withered

That little bag
Inside
Hides my secrets

I have nothing to declare
Nada that might deliver you from bondage
Nada that would keep me from coming here

My tongue cramps
Ñ
Ll

Se atrofia
No puedo
Say mas
I can't mask it any more

The magical book of my youth
Gives way to pledge of allegiance
Green, white and red
Red, white and blue

The little bag becomes a sack
The little bag becomes a trunk
The little bag becomes the globe

I have nothing to declare
The roots on my feet are snapping

Sandiegotijuana

How to sum it all up? How to explain the feeling whenever I go back? As I sat at the restaurant I saw a woman who was the older sister of a dear friend from ninth grade. I remembered some things clearly. She didn't, she wouldn't.

How not to see the bridge and remember my mother's stories of its absence. Of the ferries that took her from downtown San Diego to Coronado. How not to think of our friend the painter who for so long drove past the bridge, on his way to the campus and on his way back to the dust, and how in the end he jumped and got off.

How not to think that the changes now are the same changes of 25 years ago? What's missing now is what was missing 25 years ago.

How not to separate those fraternal twins, San Diego and Tijuana, I have my favorite. One is my best friend. One is beautiful. One I cannot do without. One I have gotten drunk with. One has given me my education, one has rubbed its fingers so hard on the streets. One is tall. One is short. One is insecure. One is a megalomaniac. One lets me put my hand under its waistband. One doesn't return my calls.

Is it the buildings or the people? Is it the people who began disappearing with the buildings? Is it the people who remind me of the buildings? Why do the buildings outlast the people?

The salty water up my nose, the Garibaldi so orange 15 feet below the surface of the water, at La Jolla Cove, and the eucalyptus in the university groves, all the coffee, all the punk rock shows, all the times

I rode that fiberglass skateboard with the thick orange wheels down the sandy boardwalk in Mission Beach. It's cement, so why do they call it a boardwalk?

All the people who owned houses my mother cleaned, whose clothes she washed, whose dishes she scrubbed, whose kids she took care of. Whose money she took. Goddamn, she worked hard.

And all the hands, arms, necks, and foreheads I touched.

And all the music made by the painters, and all the drawings made by the musicians, and all the luscious tastes served by the poets.
Yeah, I'm talking to you.

All of that, right here, right now, before the beginning is over, before the end starts.

¡Zas!

The poet said.

A Taco Shop Canto for War-Town San Diego

Land grants no more
Boom town no more
The war is no more
San Diego, war city no more
There's no need for the great wall of factories
From Pacific Highway to Kearny Mesa

General Dynamics
Solar Turbines
Jet hangars
Recruitment depots
Will all become artist lofts
Will all become free clinics
Or maquiladoras

Remember the stick floor nudie bars on Broadway
With their eighteen year-old strippers
Masquerading as world wise has been hookers
They entertained syphilis swabbies
Masquerading as eighteen year-old sharks
Ready to bite
With their babyteeth

Now Emerald Shapery
Oz-like beacon
For new industry

Has Godzilla stomped
The strip bars into the underground

Now navy-town grunge
Oozes from sidewalk cracks
Onto marble floored lobbies
Grabbing tourists by their ankles
Dragging them
Into the ground waters of free speech
And wobbly water cannon tolerance

Up the street
At Southwest Euro cafes
In Gaslamp former peep show parlors
SoCal grungified teens and twenties
Sip bites of liquified java
Posing as sidewalk billboards
With an air of falsified urbanity
And a faded touch of culpability

Fifth and Broadway
Grand central station for soultagged teens
Those who left their mark
On the shelled out Walker Scott
Glass screen
To my first fantasies of Christmas consumerism
A world size window now empty

The ghost of stock market Icarus
Falls from First National Trust

At exactly 9:00 a.m.

He falls on the Tijuana maid

Bound for La Jolla rows of mansion street

Two blocks off the route 30

Stock market Icarus

Wipes the speculation from his wings

Begs pardon from la señora

And looks progress in the face

99 cent stores

Sueño

Sek

Tmk

And other price tags

I, so-called heir apparent to the great Acosta

See all

Be all

Furiously type away

I type away the fears of my mortality

I type away the application to the pages of history

A paragraph slopped on my headstone

In some internet-sold encyclopedia delivered on CD-ROM

Call me the not-so-brown buffalo

The thirteenth generation lost leader

Call me Chintolas Jones

Nomad of Aztlan

No man

No mad Aztlan

War-town San Diego
Now Cultural Mecca in Aztlan
Has become crossroads for mestizo tonguefire
Has become crossroads for taco shop culture
Has become crossroads for chorizo tonguefire
Empty lots
No cars
Where local grunge rockers
Perform private bum-aid
For soup line empresarios gone bad
The new meeting places for push cart culture

Jetta

So many times driving under the Laurel Street Bridge. One night, I saw Manet's torero along the shoulder; two decades old, white oxford shirt with red Rorschach badges. The sheet covered his eyes. Next to him, a white Jetta, no longer moving at the speed of youth. Both made a dead stop an hour before midnight.

The New San Diego

For Paul Espinosa

Visión número uno:

Somos de nuevo México
Somos del viejo México
Somos manchas en un radar
Somos los que viven en cuevas
Somos las sirvientas

Visión número dos:

We live in a postcard world
We live in a postcard house
We work in a postcard office
Our salaries are postcard size
We go out to postcard bars
Our homies shoot each other up in postcard drive-bys
Our city hall is a postcard chamber
                with postcard vision

Visión número tres:

The border still bleeds
The maids still cross
Brown is still on the wrong side of the rainbow
OTNC still means the future

UCSD is still on a hill
South of 8 still means brown
Paul's vision still rings true
The battleships are still docked on our ass
The revolutionary whistle... led by a tequila shot

When will the next video be made
When will the next documentary be cut
When will the next down filmmaker stand up

We already have The New Tijuana
When will it be time for El Nuevo San Diego

Fifth and Broadway

Fifth and Broadway
Is more than can be said
In these four walls

Fifth and Broadway
Needs to be yelled

Fifth and Broadway
Needs to be painted
In voz alta

The victory in Europe
The victory in Japan
No victory in Vietnam

What about the victory in Barrio Logan?
What about the victory on Market Street?

The Marshall Plan for the barrio
Ends up being a blockade of opportunity

They will always win
They will always make the barrio safe
To buy houses
Not homes,
Houses

Fifth and Broadway

Needs to be screamed
For Trinidad

My aunt
Who left the best years of her life
On that bus
On that trolley
Walking
Tijuana to Mission Hills to
Tijuana to Mission Hills to
Tijuana to Mission Hills

Tia Trini couldn't work from home

Like me
Running to greet her
Carrying those check-pattern
woven plastic bags
There was always something
For everyone in there

And the crossroads
Was always Fifth and Broadway
The halfway point

Because
that's what Fifth and Broadway
Is to you and me
A point closer to your beginning
Than to your end
A place more there than here

Salvador

Sal is short for Salvador

Salvador Valtierra preaches on the corner of Fifth and Broadway
The bus depot and crossroad for pedestrian masses

This is the corner where the stock market crashed
Where Reaganomics and its cranes revived a financial district
Booming with peep-show parlors
Residence hotels and adult bookstores

Now it's the corner of ninety-nine cent stores
And ninety-nine cent lives
Lives lived out with stubby fingers
Clorox cracked skin
And tennis elbow
From pushing vacuum cleaners

Sal competes with
Incense sellers
Bow tie media moguls
Making the call
Homeless selling used bus transfers

Hip-hop pachuco taggers
Preach the gospel of sek, sueño, hem

Everyone wants to be seen

Except the maids
On their way back from five hours
Sweat bath house cleaning
The maids smell like pledge and Lysol
They sit in mourning on a bench
Waiting for the bus

The maids look forward to making
Gourmet Mexican dinners
For waiting beaks
From stale tortillas
Seasoned with used bus transfers

Sal sees the pages of testament
Written on the side of a bus
Sal feels the power of the word
A soapbox director without musicians
Sal exhales faith
For anyone willing to stop
Sal stretches his arms to embrace all

And the hip hop pachucos throw ride-by spit wads
from the half-opened windows of San Diego Transit
and wonder why Sal turns the other cheek

Field

The field of dreams
pushes the barrio.

The field of dreams
shrinks the barrio.

Union cranes
rust.

Working class pensions
dry up.

Bonds.

Redevelopment loans.

Grants.

Gentrification.

The police station
foundation
is the same
as the welfare office.

Liberty

Independence for the barrio
Freedom for the barrio

The liberty bell of the barrio
Is a car horn on a '67 Chevy

Freedom in the barrio
Is your mother's cry to come inside and eat

Freedom in the barrio
Means leaving,
saying you'll never come back
And coming back

The liberty bell of the barrio
Is a brand new car
Co-signed by Mom and Dad

The liberty bell of the barrio
Is a midnight trip to a Tijuana disco
Bare chested home boys

"Lomas"
"Diez y ocho"
"Red Steps"
"White Fence"
Pa pa pa pa pa

The liberty bell of the barrio
Is Sunday night 8 p.m. cartoons
Because Bart means freedom in Nahuatl

Lowriders leave the barrio
At night
But they always come back

The entrepreneur of the barrio
Opens a taco shop
that sells crank and mota
on the side

It's the end of an era
When Roberto's closes
When the pozole stops flowing
When the adobada stops sizzling

It's the end
When the barrio
Falls to redevelopment loans
Of urban renewal

Listen to the liberty bell of the barrio
We hang along the main streets
By our hands
By our feet

We sway back and forth
We didn't make the quota
We didn't learn English fast enough

Finca fantasies of escape
The world eats away at our skin
Like mosquitoes

And we wait for someone to cut us down
We didn't cut enough wood
We didn't get into school

Independence for the barrio

The liberty bell of the barrio
Is a car horn on a '67 Chevy

PBJH

I found my junior high school Facebook group. I jumped in and planted my flag. And declared my credentials: Kate Sessions Elementary 1976 to 1981. PBJH 1982 to 1984. Mission Bay HS 1985 to 1987. I was an undocumented Mexican kid whose mother cleaned houses on Soledad Rancho Court, Cass St., Ingraham St. and on so many others. That made me friends with the Cunninghams, the Stiskas, and made me think I was an upper middle-class, college bound kid. So much after-school time spent walking down Jewel Street during elementary school and junior high to go to the Oakwood Apartments, where my stepfather was a maintenance guy. There, I heard stories by the pool from all the World War II retired people who either fought in the war, whose family members died in the war, or who escaped anti-Semitism to stay alive. An orange, fiberglass Gordon & Smith skateboard (a leave-behind from an Oakwood apartment move out) became my hoverboard on the thin, sand-covered Mission Beach boardwalk. I wanted nothing more than to own a pair of Op cord shorts, an Op collared shirt, canvas white Nikes with the light blue swoosh. And to be able to talk to the girls. I got what I wanted. And in my senior year, 1986, guess what happened? This country said I could come out of the shadows. But a lot of other homies from those years did not come out of the shadows, and for others the shadows keep following them.

Golden Hill

Remember
big window breakfasts,
as waitress sings
Lomas alive.

Early morning light
bounces barrio
through gold-colored glasses.

Sun
comes over Palomar,
hops and skips
light
over Helix hilltops,
double crosses mesa tops.

Children
learn to roll
geyser-steaming tortillas,
tender fingertips
burn,
but do not callous.

Coffee,
potatoes,
eggs,
orange juice.

Kids
hold menu
Sinai tablet-like.

At our table
it's a breakfast
of the morning after
the forties party,
the Tijuana concert party,
the fish in the oven party.

The hours don't stop.
Morning becomes
an afternoon of obligations

futból,
beisból,
couch.

Sixteenth Street

You must keep looking
For the one who called it
The Sixteenth Street Renaissance
The one who came up with the name

Under coats of paint
You'll find
Chabalaba
Alexandria of coffeeshops
Kitch
Chabachinos
And Charo

During midnight AM/PM meetings
Allen warned me
Write your first draft
Because it may be your last

Not far
A baseball bar
Crossroads for geometry and statistics
Now home to soup lines
Down and out
Taken care by God's extended hand

Enjoy it
Because the landlord's grip doesn't slip

Jewel Box
Cleaned up grunge bar
Two bullet holes
Look for them
As I drag you out the back door

Six year old Clarita
Watches from her bedroom window upstairs

In between
Straight-aheads gone bad
Back to the dark side

GTM
Is the new Woolworth
Is the new Walker Scott
Will be the old 99 cent story
Retail food
Second hand food
Preservative-free clothes

The jacarandas are months away
From waking up
The bears of sixteenth settle in for a long sleep

The wind blows from City College
Towards Market Street
And Gilbert's trumpet doesn't answer

They called it the 16th street renaissance
Chabalaba,

Alexandria of coffeeshops
Kitch
Chabachinos and Charo as barista

Midnight AM/PM meetings
When Allen warned me
Write your first draft
Because it may be your last

Straight aheads gone bad
To the dark side

Wrestle

I wrestled
the 24 year-old me
down C Street,
past the Stevie Ray Vaughan mural,
we landed on 16th Street,
I tore his Aztec necklace
and swallowed it.

I wrestled
the 14 year-old me,
on Fiberflex skateboards
on Mission boardwalk sand.

I ripped
his brown Op cord shorts
down Ingraham Street,
flipped off Mr. P
for that "F" in English.

The three of us:
two younger me's
and me doing
full nelson
camel clutch
sunset flip
pile drivers

as we tumbled
on the Coronado bridge
back to Chicano Park.

The border
didn't stop us.
The Mexican migra man ran after me
Where were... all of you born?

Isn't it obvious,
I pointed to the cactus.

Move along.

My younger selves
saw that I passed the test,
changed my name.

You're now Salvador!

Salgo de dónde
la sal go,
tu sales, el sale,
nosotros salimos.
Sal si puedes
Sal va vidas
Sal si te dan ganas.

Has it been
forty seconds,
forty days,

or forty years?
Looking, waiting,
at the edge of the land
I want to enter,
next to a sign that says:
DF-TJ-NC-SD-LA-LB-DF-TJ-NC-SD-LA-LB.

We moved laterally
into the waves,
got caught in fishing lines
from the Imperial Beach pier.

Kept wrestling to the wall,
saw an opening,
followed the wind, the mist, the butterflies,
through.

Jacob got a better name.

Mine only means
Struggles with Spanish
Struggles with English
Struggles with absent father
Struggles with fatherless mother
Struggles to remember the final score
Struggles with green, white, and red
Struggles with the red, white, and blue

We stop
dust off the pieces
and kiss each other on the cheek.

On the Opening of the New National City Public Library

Our history is written in 19th century journals
Our history is written in cholo script in an alley behind St. Anthony's
Our history is written on the sandy banks of the reservoir
Remember the artist who destroyed all his art

They brought their books
To the rancho de la nación

Protestant chanting streams out of the Bay Theater and into the
harbor

The library was the sanctuary
The library kept me inside, and took me out

Children still play among the mountains of recycled metal
A boy opens a book and dreams

Underneath 8th Street you can still hear the chanting of the Torah

The train tracks came and went
The night clubs and pizza parlors came and went
The Navy ships will have come and gone
The mile of cars will one day be a yard of tires
But the people will have their books
But the people will have their language
But the people will have their stories

A girl opens a book and dreams

One day, the house with the best view will be the one atop Mt. San
Miguel

We have lived to see the day when the books get their rightful
repository

Rise Raza
Wise up people

George's cakes will become a taqueria, will become Manila fried
chicken, will become a pupuseria, will become a union hall, will
become an overseas call center for Chinese credit card companies

Don't touch the words because they are holy
Devour the words because they are holy

Read to the children
So they can leave
And come back

There's a railroad diary buried there
There's a Bible buried there
There's a Torah buried there
There's a Koran buried there

And the water we have cast
Has sprouted these new walls
So that a little boy and a little girl
Can open up a book and dream

Boom Town National City

National City is where I laid my head down on a rock to sleep. It's where I rode my avocado green three-speed bike. It's where the scrap metal yards form a mountain of blessings and a mountain of curses. It's where a studio apartment on McKinley, in Old Town National City, led to three homes for my mother and stepfather. How can that be? How can two immigrants, two refugees of fatherlessness and lovelessness, two asylum seekers from worlds they couldn't fit into, end up owning three homes? Blind work, weekend work, living like the poor, not consuming, but spending. Did they do anything wrong? You bet. Just ask my brother and sister. National City is where I slept, but from where I left when it was time to go to school. My mother cleaned five houses in the same neighborhood so my Pacific Beach school uniform was Op cord shorts and a Lightning Bolt shirt. My chariot was a fiberglass G&S skateboard with knobby orange wheels that played a different 33 ⅓ melody on the sandy Mission Beach boardwalk Monday through Friday than they did on the bumpy sidewalks next to Kimball Park on Saturday and Sunday.

I learned to be a Chicano while living and leaving National City. Chicano history was all around me but I didn't know it. When I was ten, Herman Baca fought for self-determination through the Committee on Chicano Rights, in National City. That's when he said to the President: the detention of children is barbaric!

Mt. San Miguel, what is the name, please somebody tell me the mountain's Kumeyaay name. Is it the love of your mother? Is it the love of your father?

Mt. San Miguel is the eastern gate of National City, a mountain that opens and lets the morning sun through. The mountain is a tombstone and a launching pad in National City. Mt. San Miguel has a twin, Cerro del Cubilete in Guanajuato, the dead center of Mexico. El Cerro was my mother's mountain, topped by a stone statue of Christ after the religious civil war. Guanajuato in National City. My mother's father, Miguel (not making it up), saw the Guanajuato mountain before Christ stood atop it. Maybe it was the last thing Miguel saw before he was killed. He was 23 years old, the last of the 17 kids. He shook the tree for land. His father had plenty but that was 15 kids earlier. Maybe Miguel realized he deserved more when he sojourned in New York, winter 1945. So his grandson is to live in the shadow of the mountain from six years old until he's 23, until his stepfather threatens to kill him during a drunken rage.

It was right around the time I finished UCSD, a few months before the graduation ceremony. One of these days I'm going to ask for my transcripts from UCSD just to remember how close I came, in National City, to falling into the mouth of the deep brown earth. In one of the ancient stories the protagonist sleeps on a rock and wakes in a way he had never done before. He says to the source of all creation: okay, if I make it, if I get what I want, I will follow you, I will believe in the oneness of all creation.

Well, guess what motherfuckers? I got it. Our beloved protagonist makes it. Builds. Loves. Ruins everything. Earns. Spends. Saves. Comes back to National City, sees the rock on which he dreamed, remembers the promise he made.

He wants to believe. It is so hard to believe.

I spent 17 years before the mast in National City. That mast was the Bay Theater's tower. All the way to the bay, it seemed to say on National City Boulevard. Wind - yes, wind - not a quake, not God's hand, not a carefully planted bomb tumbled, pushed down, made the tower flaccid. The same wind disappeared the Italian pizza joint on National City Boulevard and Eighth Street with the show off dough-twirler in the window.

The same wind turned the Hebrew Day School on 8th Street into some kind of Stratford Upon Avon-architectural detail strip mall. There was Torah taught there, across from the 19th century church with beautiful wood beams.

You want 19th century? National City's got 19th century and 20th century post-war middle-class grids. The ones John Baldessari knew well when he told you how not to take a picture, or how not to create art. He burned everything. He promised: no more boring art. And for one moment he stayed, he settled, kids and art and all, in National City.

To all the girls I tried to kiss in National City: I'm sorry I didn't have the words to talk or explain. I've got something better now. I have the questions.

I found questions in the stacks of the National City Public Library. I lived a block away for nine years. Listen to this one: I started going to the stamp club with my messed up stamps from Mexico. I was eleven. A member of the club - all old and retired, Anglo guy with a 1950s pepper gray - was touched, did a good deed and paid my dues. He made me a stamp tribe made man. Then the people where my mother worked (Holocaust survivors, Methodist missionaries, children of Polish Catholic immigrants living the upper middle class dream) started giving me stamps from their collection. So I walk into the club one day, this Mexican kid flashing his badass stamps. And the retireds throw their WTF emoji faces in a FB Live splash.

There's a liberty bell in the National City barrio. It's the car horn on a burgundy '79 stick shift Nova my stepfather drove off the Pontiac lot. Does that mean anything to you, the Pontiac lot on the Mile of Cars? How about the Mile of Bars? C'mon, will the real drinking town borrachos and Tom Waits wannabes please stand up?

Emo took over National City in 1985. Yeah, man. The Gonzales family: three daughters and a son. They were my Jalisco family next door. The kids outnumbered the parents. They knew how to count votes. In my house my mother outnumbered everyone. She knew how to count votes. Brother Carlos turned me on to New Order, Siouxie, Depeche. I hope turning you on to Caifanes was payback enough.

Up the street from our 8th Street home the sun glistens on the skinny-dipping pool in the hills in National City. Yes, National City has a "Heights". National City has people who move on up and stay.

These days, brother Xavier lives and posts National City as he takes walks between the mountains of blessings and curses. They will always be there. National City is a continuous emanation. Your skin needs it but it can harm you. National City is-es without stop: past, present, and future. Give me some of your Vitamin D Avenue. I need it. I want it. But don't burn, cuz like Los Illegals said, we don't need a tan.

I fell in love with a bird that came and rested on a branch in National City. The bird asked me to fall asleep with it. I did. But when we woke I couldn't say words the bird could understand. So the bird took me to the bush with flowers dripping nectar, above where the bird's father lay dead. I tried to drink the nectar but could not and I did not understand that the bird took me there so that I could teach the bird how to mourn and leave. Now a DM is all we have to sing each other songs of gratitude.

Follow me: in a total time vision tectonic plates rub skin, get off on each other and in millennial orgasms birth the bay, Mt. San Miguel, and creeks that carry silt on their backs time and again through rainy seasons that tick like the second hand. So much silt brought from the mountains' inner thighs it makes the bay shallow enough for you to walk on. You can walk on water in National City. But lose faith in yourself and you sink. Hold on long enough and you'll reach the other side. Underground railroad arms wait.

Do you remember when the Mexican American mayor said, yes of course National City is a sanctuary city. It's as if he drove west on Division, floored it, rammed that huge "psychic" sign high over the freeway, it fell on him and instead of a halo of chirping birds and stars, he saw the Hebrew words:

גֵּר־וְתוֹשָׁב אָנֹכִי עִמָּכֶם

You know: ger vetoshav anochi imachem. It's Abraham's big reveal as

he's looking for a burial place for his beloved and says to the Hittite:
within me is a sojourner, asylum seeker, outsider AND a resident.
Let's look at each other, comrade, we are both from here and not
from here.

And then the white mayor took over; and in a Frank Kimball voice
said, hell's to the muthafuckin no this ain't no sanctuary city. Wassa
matta, Frank, compassion gonna make you late for church? Let me
let you in on a little secret, Frank. National City has been a sanctuary
for sojourners, the ones from Hopkinton, Chandler, Lipa City, Tecun
Uman, Jerez, Romita, those towns in Denmark and the Tyrol too.
National City's not unique. It doesn't only happen here.

Listen to the dream. Here it comes:
It's the Maytime band review, turning the corner from 12th Street
onto the Kimball Park amphitheater. Fourteen-year old me in my
bedroom has no clue this is the day, gets up out of bed at noon to see
the boys and girls, like me, with their batons, their sousaphones, their
pom poms. The boys with their fade haircuts, the girls march their
brown legs and make the pleats bloom. The boys on the trumpets
pucker up and blow just enough under the noon sun to give you
heatstroke. These are suburban Chicanos, like Oscar Gomez Jr., the
ones who played little league far from the barrio, not immigrants
like me.

Following behind the marching band: the bouncing Impalas play,
"Ooh Boy (I Love You So)."
It's like that James Ensor painting, *Christ's Entry into Brussels in
1889*: people in calavera masks, in gluttony masks, the bishop more

a clown than a band leader. And Jesus on a burro, a needle in a haystack.

The music from the band and the lowriders bring out the people from their two-story apartment buildings. They wear *papier-mâché* masks: a devil with a whip, the bull, a woman, el borracho, and the drum and fife. Green, white, and red streamers and banners drop from a nopal that appears about 50 feet above the band. What has its talons digging into the cactus's flesh? You guessed it: an eagle devouring a snake. But the nopal keeps moving with the band, doesn't stay still.

Another band follows the lowriders. It's from Katella in Anaheim. It's the ones who won the trophy last year, the year eleven died as they tried to outrun the Border Patrol. The kids can't take the deaths and prepare an alternate song, one they practiced on their own time, unknown to the music director. Just as they approach the dignitaries in coats and tails, they play Sensemaya by Silvestre Revueltas, the part near the end that sounds like the uprising of the mahogany plantation workers as they overthrow and kill their plantation masters like in the book by B. Traven. The cymbals, the brass, the flags say, we will not be hanged by our feet, by our hands.
All the National City Sir Topham Hatts' eyes bulge, become bloodshot. They know the message: time's up! The band doesn't miss a beat.

Why am I telling you all this? I have no choice. It's what I lived in National City. I'm handing off the baton. You and I hold it for a moment. I ask, you got it? You wonder, do I have it? And then you take off like the fabulous self that you are.

Fill your fountain pen with blood, fill it with the rainbow ink sliding down the corner of your eye. Write your own postcard. Write it multiple times. Write it when you love. Write it when you're lonely. Write it when you feel that you're returning to your original self, your whole self.

Write it when things happen that make you cry.

And wake up!

National City is where 1986 lifted an undocumented weight off me and my parents. And where it fell 32 years later like a boulder on the corner of 24th and D Avenue on top of three girls seeing their mother dragged into a migra truck by three men. Were the agents trying to pull the mother's arms and legs out of their sockets? Stand on that corner and you'll feel the girls' screams rise like subway exhaust out from under the sidewalk. Are they wails? Are they the sound of vocal chords snapping? Are they declarations of the self-evident? We do not deserve to be treated this way! We are human beings!

Should we carve an image out of basalt of a dismembered woman and embed it at that corner?

For now, it's another point on the map made of fig and mulberry fibers. It's the map of detentions, of the crying, of the separation, of the centers, and of the hangings.

The 1840s map of National City, the one that says we as white men have the authority to say this is the beginning, rests in a library in Berkeley. Look at the Sierra de San Miguel, el Arroyo de San Miguel, el camino para la frontera. Juan Foster claims the rancho.

Somewhere on that map, in ink made invisible by the wind, are the Kumeyaay words: his name wasn't Juan, it was John and all those Spanish words don't even come close to our eternal words for the land. The Kumeyaay words say, do not kill each other over the land.

The night I left National City in 1993 is my beginning of time. My stepfather's threat birthed my first day in my first month. I left in a rush, out of the funnel, squeezed through. How did I get out of there? How long did it take?

I found a home on a golden hill and didn't look back on National City until the library called on me to write a poem. It's there, you can read it on a plaque next to the elevator in the National City Public Library. It has these lines:
Read to the children
So they can leave
And come back

Lost Professors

This is for our friends who escaped the So Cal waves of gentrification
This is for our friends, warriors against barrio violence, bringing
peace to Eastern shores
This is for our friends, who headed east to find Mexican flags
hanging from tenements

We are the lost professors
We are the students talking to the burning bush
We are the ones who talk to ourselves
We are the 20 year-olds found in Buddhism
                            found in homosexuality
                            found in poverty
                            found in mortgage payments

We are the 30 year-olds found in 2 a.m. bars
            found talking Chicano liberation and 401Ks
            found in madness by the fork in the road
            found in second marriages
            found in darkness

Did Chicano Park cost as much as a web page?
Did People's Park cost as much as a web page?
Did Wounded Knee cost as much as a web page?

A Sound Yo-Yo Man Y Fiesto

Yo manifiesto
that the sounds of the border
continue to ricochet
between my ears.

The merolicos of Mexico City
follow me north,
folding tables set up
at the MacArthur Park red line station.

They yell
the pochteca
chants of commerce,
same ones ringing
up and down the Americas,
for thousands of years.

Listen to the wall,
what sound does it make?

Listen to the freeway,
what accent can you hear?

Forget the images of housekeepers,
brown skinned politicians
and blond crossover
Mexican singers.

Close your eyes,
listen to the sounds
skip down the sidewalk.

Listen to the Morse Code
of people's heels.

The Muslim father
in East Hollywood
tells his son:
"God gave you two ears,
and one mouth.
Listen twice
as much
as you speak."

Encinitas

The sand is hard because the ocean water turns powder solid. The waves' last life tumbles the rocks. Even soft stones scrape blood from the skin that covers my bones. I step and avoid the rocks, but I can't see where I step when the waves and their foam and the brown cloud of sand inside the wave covers the rocks. I keep walking. Stepping on a smooth stone can still hurt. I like how cold the ocean water feels on my skin.

Vine a Los Angeles

The eagle
perched on the cactus
called me to Los Angeles.

The Templo Mayor lays buried here.

In my city,
Mexico City,
jaguar heads of volcanic stone
became cornerstones for colonial palaces,
became podiums for politicians,
became baptism wells for el nuevo mexicano.

In my new city
adobe forts
became foundations
for post-war tract homes,
as far as the eye can see.
They sway
like Kansas wheat fields.

It's here,
the Californio city
buried
under the oil well city
buried
under the Zoot Suit city

buried
under the Dunbar city.

Orthodox shuls
under Brooklyn Avenue
sonidero speakers.

The Eastside minaret
blasts narcocorridos.
The Eastside minaret
blasts Cri Cri.

The Eastside minaret
Blasts na-na-na-na-na-na-na-na-na-na-na.

Cross
the river
over forearms graffiti-tattooed.

The frogs
sleep under the concrete.
The rows of grape vines
sleep under the concrete.
The boom-booms from
the Masque,
the Vex,
and the Moratorium
sleep under the concrete.

Use your hands,
dig deep.

Use your nose,
dig deep.
Use your mouth,
dig deep.
Use your heart,
dig deep.

The Movement

I saw the heirs to the great movement
divided by the 150 year-old legacy
of isolation fear dangerous oppression.

I saw the great Chicano minds
bickering over the whiteness of their skin.

I saw the heirs to Emma, Corky, Reies, and Jose Angel
waiting for the spoils of handout government cheese-
already rotten in the refrigerator of white America-

I saw the history books
which we had begun to write in the 1960s
erased by the hands
of the moral and assimilationist majority
and by our Hispanic governors and other politicians.

I saw these same history books
used as firewood in the fireplace of white America.

I saw the brightest Chicano minds of my generation
put war paint on their faces,
leave their knowledge behind
and make the pilgrimage to the capital of Aztlan,
BURNING.

I saw the great Chicana women

fighting for their place in a divided and sexist movement,
being told not to divide
and to get some cafecito mi amorcito.

I saw the great Chicano minds
go through the mechanized garbage disposal education system
come out with many Ks in their paychecks
and with an amnesia of Hispanic proportions.

That's the black plague I saw.

I saw the great Chicano Shamen of my generation
shave their heads in desperation
and go into exile to the country that was once theirs,
the great MESHICO,
now taken away by the mispronunciation
of "tecnócratas solidarios educados en gringolandia"
new home to liberal economics, and McBurritos
around the corner from the Zocalo.

And in a side street, Anystreet,
five cops wait for night raid on Chicano house
looking for heroin among the medicine bottles
of a newly operated señora waiting to search
in Estelita and Luisita's vagina
for the rocks that kill us.

And instead of 6,000 activists that August day
I saw the soldiers of la Raza
lined up on each side of the Appian Way Whittier Boulevard

crucified five feet apart for miles
with acupuncture syringes on their bodies,
each Sebastian an unwilling martyr
hanging from the bus stop sign
and the sodium light lamp post.
The needles made a Guadalupe aura.

I saw their hands through the bars of hopelessness,
their futures as sirvientas, busboys, mechanics
and third-rate actors made me weep.

At the base of each cross
three taxpayers crouched
gambling away the belongings of each victim,
a cascade jacket, a mascada, a hairnet, and a cruz,
and the title to the land grant Rancho de las Californias
now Rodeo Drive.

The Capital of Aztlan Burns

In patria chica San Diego
The llantos of Rolando Rey
Reach me at the speed of sound
Batter my swollen eyes
Electrocute
Repeatedly

Los cotorros de la televisión
Plead for reservists
To report to stations
Güera's voice oscillates
Fear
Desperation
Terror
Instinctive protection
Accorralados como bestias

Palmeras brought for 1932 Olympics
Sunglasses melt
Palm trees burn
Sol, arena, sangre

Seeping out of the streets
Of fantastic Losangelestitlán
Lined with flaming
Heretic

Palms
A pastel light of vice
Velas de luto
Around el féretro losangelino

Arrival

Mari came out from San Anto,
big river suitcase
dreams by her side.

She wanted to doctor
the kids back to life,
one classroom at a time.

Sacred heart, all the way.

Wanted to find her place
in the rainbow of brown.

She'd heard
how the river changed its course here,
wanted to see it happen again,
wanted to feel the rain
slide down the foothills
and flood
down her back.

Spent her first east side sunset
on the second floor balcony
listening
to the little guitars
the five green neon letters
blazing

their call to prayer,
"Sra. Es" they repeated.

This was the home
she searched for.

Between classes and finals
she found time for marches.

Mari was the real deal,
down and brown,
fist up high.

The year before she defended,
between Sunday night sambas,
took her to the garden,
the central place
south of the city.

We walked
skin to the earth
acre after acre,
her ankles brushed the leaves,
epazote,
calabazas,
corn.

This is where all could learn.
The sunset was no longer a mystery.
The shades of yellow, orange, and red,
clear patterns, made by the wind,

the watercolor hand, the drying light.

That's where Mari met Tizoc.
They wove their fingers
into a basket,
cradled hearts.

The thin blades from the corn
whipped by the Santa Anas,
cut short gashes in their arms.

It was all too much,
lots of kids
lots of casualties,
making little progress.

Mari dropped out.
Mari plugged in
and moved to the garden.

She slept under a canopy
of upside down yellow trumpets.

Last time I saw her
she was on the other side of a spewing
bulldozer
come to clear the place.
Our eyes locked as we remembered.

Mari laid it all on the line,
she lied down in front of that machine

made like the outline
of that mountain volcano.
Everyone else did too.

Her comadre
wrapped her legs around a tree.

That was a decade ago
when Mari drank that six o'clock sunset
and battled for you and me.

Neighborhood

My song says my city is a plot of rich earth in the middle of a forgotten lake. My LA neighborhood is Peralvillo in Mexico City where I was born, the apartment where my mother, father and I lived, its walls, its love, dried up, like the lake. My LA neighborhood is Colonia Aleman, Tijuana where my single mom and I looked over the cliff, at night, to the fields of San Ysidro: the fence, the border birds circling, our toes touched the edges, the soil crumbled beneath us. My LA neighborhood is 1986 M-F Amnesty, that said for a brief moment, no human is illegal. Then the door shut. Again. It is every single corner and sidewalk where I've stood and held my microphone, talking to people en las buenas y en las malas, that's my LA neighborhood. It's Beaudry, where the teachers shut the street down, handcuffed into police buses. It's the second floor on Gage and Cesar Chavez. Me, recien-llegado reporter in 2000, and Ofelia Esparza talking about her altar made of the flower petals of our migrant footsteps. It's Mt. Sinai, Forest Lawn, where I accompanied for burial and said Kaddish for brother Joe Lissack, Roosevelt High, class of '52. I love you, all you beautiful LA people. Because I need all of you; all are a sliver of creation. When I said all of you, I meant all of you. Why do I feel this way? Because I heard my eulogies, at my LA neighborhood on Third and Pine, Long Beach, May 31, 2020. The chants that day: "don't shoot, we love Long Beach." I interviewed, I reported. Police shot a foam round that hit the bottom of my neck. My eulogy: I can breathe. My eulogy: you can breathe. What am I going to do with that breath? Heal. What are you going to do with your breath?

Nooks

The light fades
In the hills
Canyon houses fear no sunset
Except the ones at the top

Silverlake L.A.
Two tax brackets away
From Salvatrucha Echo Park

Four B-Boys walk
To the river's mouth

Palm trees stretch
For a glimpse of the green flash

But we're at the foot of the canyon
Fear not the dying of the light

Pine trees climb
On top of junipers

The nooks
The hills in any city
The views

The houses with views
The houses on the hills
In any city

Contain the same breakfast nooks

Tepid coffee
Warm orange juice
Cold kisses

While pine trees climb
On top of junipers

Rios Cars

Roads on stilts
Crossroads
River of cars

I got out to meet the man who was bathing
Under the overpass

I got out of my car because
it wasn't important to get to work on time
I got out of my car because half-a-mile back
An eighteen-wheeler
hit the space I was driving in
Random
I got out of my car
because the man may have the answer

Praise the river
Full in spring
Trickling in summer

You begin as snow
Now carry lead
Now carry chromium
Now carry 10W40
Now carry the confessions of man

River

Road
Burdened
Leave man's sins in my pores

I praise you
I worship our path
I give you my strength

Exaltada seas
Como en los tiempos antes del offramp
Como en los tiempos de mud dams

Es sábado hijo
Escucha el ronroneo del corazón
Cuatro cilindros

Belmont

These streets hide
too many footsteps
these streets hide
too many tears.

Walk the streets, hear the people
who came before.

Oil wells foundations for homes.
Oil wells the greed of industry.
Oil wells cradle our children.

In the distance the cathedral
rises lit up by future light.

Oil wells outlive the children.
Oil wells play with the children.
Oil wells breathe with the children.
Oil wells sleep with the children.

At night downtown; beacon, a light bulb to the moths.

There mexicanos and centroamericanos
lift the Guadalupe, Monte de Calvario,
lift the Guadalupe, Iwo Jima.

Props and all, Guadalupe appears
to Juan Diego Mulholland at seven thirty every morning

on his walk to
the hall of justice, suited up.

Guadalupe appears to Maria de Lourdes Stearns at half an hour
before midnight, every night in the lobby of marble high rise
as she clocks in to push vacuum cleaners.

The Guadalupe aura on city hall
does Coyolxauhqui battle with Huitzilopochtli.

Her light bounces off the springs on Barrington.
Her light parallel bars on the Lorena Street bridge.
Her light a drip down Western.
Her light bursts from the Sepulveda dam.

The people will walk from the hills.
The people will walk from the canyons.
The people will walk from the cul-de-sacs.
The people will walk from the foothills.

Gather around city hall, white shirts.

They samba, they twerk,
they dance a quebradita,

And at the same time, all inhale
a collective "cool"

And when they're back in the hills, when they're back
in the canyons, oil wells start back up again.

Oil wells bells, when it's time to pray.

Oil wells jalando dinero del subsuelo.
A la ruru niña duérmase mi ya.
A la ruru niño duérmase mi ya.

Maus Haus

Caridad
Holds hand
Walks home from first grade
On Union street

She looks east
Cranes fly
Lay down silver sheets

Another crane
Flies between
Bunker hill buildings

Silver sheet
Falls like blanket
Skin on symphony
Skeleton

Father says,
That's where los músicos will play

Caridad:
Why are they covering it?
Why don't they leave it open?
So the notes can fly
Be free

That night
Caridad prays to a picture of Revueltas
Begs the violins,
the bassoons and the kettledrums
be heard in the barrio

Revueltas appears
Like a blimp Guadalupe atop Bunker Hill

A crowd starts to form
They stop shopping at La Curacao, and walk downtown
They stream over the river
On the Spring Street Viaduct
On the First Street Bridge
The Fourth Street Bridge
They wade through the river and walk up the banks

In Santa Monica Frank Gehry gets a call:
"Sylvestre Revueltas is tearing the roof off the concert hall with a can
opener!"

Revueltas
Lets the notes run down Grand Avenue
Lets them fly over Temple Street
Lets them fall into the gutter and drain into the river

The quarter notes skip to the taco truck to eat a torta
The sharp notes dance norteño
with the janitors heading to the skyrises
The flat notes ride see saw on the oil wells near Belmont

Caridad says
This is better than church
I wish the music would stay

Prudent

Beaudry
would've tagged
Français-pride
placazos
starboard
Rodin's craggy rock.

Balzac
harrumphs
at waves of Wilshire
women.

He's a pot-belly
frantic
scribe
among the palms.

Vignes
slavishly
brags
about his thousand
barrels of wine.

Now crumbled
bread-like.

Evening

The outline
of the houses against the sky.

Mother holds you by
the hand. Father leads the way
to the storefront church.

De un lado los caballeros,
del otro lado las damas.

On time, Hermano Tulio opens
the prayer book.
Praise him for what we have.
Praise him for what we don't have.
Demos gracias
porque hay otro mundo
mejor que este.

The church, a hole in the window,
bigger than a bullet.

Today we rest. Today we wait for
tomorrow's aches.

On this corner dresses fall
below the ankle.
On this corner it's a festival of flesh.

Demos gracias a Dios que
superamos nuestras tentaciones.
Praise him for controlling our desires.

On this corner la señora pulls
her daughter's hand.
The girl will be the second Chicana mayor.

On this corner obreros
walk up stairs seeking just compensation
for the lost hand, for the crushed ankle.

On this corner, a street poet doesn't
stand a chance against the street preacher
turning his lungs inside out against Satanás.

La palabra de Diós en esta tierra, hermanos
luchamos contra el mal. Es la hora
de la redención escuchen a Jesucristo, que murió en el Calvario
Dejen la cocaina
Dejen la heroina
Dejen de fornicar
El tiempo se acaba
Salven a sus hijos

Cars pass, a Rolls with
the steering wheel on the right side.

The buses on a Sunday night, full.
The niños in the back seat
next to the couple fondling each other.

He's digging his face into her chest

Hey, soy de El Salvador.
The tattoo is for my father
who died on my 33rd birthday.
He loved roses so I tattooed a rose bush
on my ankle.

As you see, it comes up to my thigh.
Look at how it blooms when it
reaches the corner, follow it back
with your eyes, to the roots
on the soles of my feet.

Trucks

Potenza, Cocenza, Foggia, Bari, Catania, Kiev... and Cambodian towns, and Vietnamese towns, and the towns of Idaho, and Iowa, and the towns of Wisconsin, along with Tecolotlan, Magdalena, La Sauceda, Zapopan, Romita, Sombrerete, County Cork, Dalat, Tay Ninh.

These names. Utter these names. Whisper these names in Brentwood daylight. Chant these names at Broadway protests. Scream these names on Whittier Boulevard marches.

Say these names to praise the soil. Say these names to document the passage. Say these names to remember the trek. Say the names of the towns. Obliterate the names of the towns.

Write them on your trucks, hold them on the tip of your tongue. The names of the towns, the little towns, the ranches, wear the names between your eyes, remember them when you rise up and when you lie down. Remember them when you are away.

These names are on the trucks, seen through weed wackers, rakes, lawnmowers, shovels, and plastic trash bins.

The names are amulets at work. The names are out of reach. The names are out front. The names are small. The names are cursive. The names disappear. I don't know the names.

You've seen the trucks
Some Chevys

Some Fords
Some all fucked up

Weed wackers hanging from the side
Like a labrador lapping up the air
Lawnmowers in back
Ladders hung from home-welded racks

The hometown names on bumpers, on windows

All come to remake
the hometown here
Only better

Third & Witmer

The vatos at Third and Witmer
Form a V with their shoes
It's not the Venceremos Brigade

The lobby of the three-story apartment
Three doors
Industrial strength locks
Keep out

An iron mesh
Stocking. Transparent
Estan en la jaula

It's a quarter to three on a Thursday in January
The afternoon
Enjaulados
Bleached undershirts
Ese
Handshake
We don't need a bag for the bottle
The señoras push their strollers
Past the caged lion exhibit

These vatos pass the bottle
Eighteen year olds
Some bar mitzvah age
As the street slows and speeds with cars and bicycles

The vatos on Third and Witmer
Their hands in black gloves

Evergreen and Brooklyn

One year ago
A night shower swept me down Evergreen

Ahora regreso
Looking for that elusive grain of gold
It was November second

La huesera follows me
She unfolds her table next to El Grano de Oro
She soothes backs, hunched over
She relieves el estress
She presses out hope cramps

Evergreen and Brooklyn
The tamborazo lures me in
A Chicano charmer is on accordion

The showers swept Boyle Heights
The showers
try to dissolve Breed Street shul into the river
No se puede

Huesera curame
Huesera ten piedad de mi
Huesera quiereme mucho
Huesera ayuda a mis hijos

I warned my friends on Ford
The rains are coming this way
Find shelter in the mortuary

The marigolds
Sliver up your nose
It's a wake-up aroma sliding down your throat

At Evergreen and Brooklyn
Los homies
carved out a three-language Rosetta Stone

La huesera prays in front of the wall
The señoras get off the Sunset line
Stop and kneel

There must be an answer there
There must be a question there
Las señoras prayed louder and louder
So those sleeping could hear

But the tamborazo
Kept on playing
And drowned out the cries of sorrow

Primera Caida/the 2006 Marches

This is my song to the city

Gente wrapped themselves in white
Gente wrapped themselves in red white and blue
Gente wrapped themselves in red white and green

No Niños Héroes here

Millions, each one of them,
looks straight into
the face of Mr. and Mrs. America

You are my other self

When they're done
they swell the bridges

The First Street bridge
The Fourth Street bridge
The Sixth Street bridge

The sun slides,
follows the Northern prophet
both board a bus.
"In A Sentimental Mood"
plays as they cross the bridge

As they walk back

they ask,
let me see your tongue

Pink

White-coated

Obsidian

Hairy

Obscene

Bitter

Forked

Treacherous

Came

To this city many years ago

led by promises of work
and dreams and sun, after leaflets dropped
on my postcard town.

Here, the sun steams the dew,
and the factory whistle calls.

Inside, the boss says, good work and
keep it up.
Outside they say, go back.

These mountains, rivers, and sunsets
still a second language to me.

Your pictures of great grannies
in flappers' hats became my own.

Outsider, a name for someone else.

Dreams of my town, when mother's
calloused hand let go of mine.

Your fingers curl around
my knuckles: fastball, sinker, slider and curve.

Some years turned into more, my friends

said, don't stay too long.

We looked each other eye to eye,
took a step onto the bridge.

Below, the dry river bed
the protests

        the rents
        the raves
        and the past.

We stared at the now,
looked at the moment,
and blinked at the present, caught
inside the space made by
my palm and yours.

In My Time Here

In my time here I listened to the Mexican American Mayor who
remembers the Chicano lawyer who ran for Sheriff promising
to eliminate the office, the Chilean exile who saves dropouts on
Skid Row, the longshore worker from Wilmington who said "those
wetbacks," the cycling Dreamer with the big 'ol bigote, the ranchera
singer from Tucson whose eyes well up because Mexico betrayed
him, his gay son, the Argentinian cyclists at the velodrome, the
27-year-old councilman who learned from the elder-statesman to
count to eight, the lexicon barber, the 1980s radio reporter who
was welcomed to his new job with a, "get that Mexican off the air,"
the Cal State L.A. graduate fitted with boxing gloves and pink
wrapping around her knuckles, the Downey college grad who
lives in her car who talked to me about her film about a Cuban
American lesbian aspiring photojournalist with a lust for bi-women
and malt liquor, the East L.A. Japanese Americans who have tias in
Tijuana, the filmmaker who believes brown is the new green, the
Tijuana grunge promoter doing business in South Central, the state
political kingmaker with too much dirty laundry to come home, the
Guatemalan woman with a football son at Fairfax High School,
the CDMX exiles who strum their home into being with trova, the
former Chihuahua gold miner who drops his sack 'o rocks at 514 S.
Spring Street, the Lincoln High second year senior who ignores her
gang family, the undocumented college graduate who weaves plastic
bags into money and dreams she's a salmon, the cathedral doors'
sculptor born in Mexico City, the Blaxican rapper, the Nicaraguan
woman who won't say the word negro, the Puerto Rican model and

The Maybelline Girls, the musicians who use jaranas instead of light sabers, and more times than I want to count, the radio reporter from CDMX, Tijuas, and San Diego who roams the streets of Los looking for the right words for the sounds he hears.

Primero de mayo del 2010

For Shifra Goldman

RO JOE ROW JOE JOB HOW NOW BOW CRIMSON
RED ROVER BLED BLOOD YIDDISH BEGINS MIDDLE
ENGLISH MIDDLE SPANISH YIDDISH ENDS I AM
STEAM RISES NEW YORK GO WEST LANDS PALMS
JEREMIAH LIES JEREMIAH BURIED BLOW TRUMPET
SLEEPY LAGOON TRUMPET POLICE CLUBS FLY DEFEND
VATOS

Today's portion is about the sin offering
Today's portion is about the burnt offering
Today's portion is about the rituals for the new temple
Today's portion is about a half-breed who sins

We bid the Sabbath goodbye
People stream over the bridges
Back from the march
Pebbles stuck on stroller wheels

Five words about Siqueiros:

fist
fight
jail
cartucho

blood

Nananana nazizona hey hey goodbye
Nananana nazizona hey hey goodbye

Five words about Yreina's mural under the Beverly bridge:

Dolores
huelga
eagle
dying
mother
aerosol

She sees the shadow
Of the crucified Indian
Brings others

Workers still lose hands
eyes
               feet
        in the factories

Five words about The Wall That Cracked Open:
knife
bread
¡Ya!
brother
placazo

When a mural goes up on the Eastside

Shifra's there

When miners are exploited and die

Shifra is there

When government asks you to double-cross

Shifra is there

To say "No!"

The Cornet on Western and Adams

For William Pajaud

This is for Pajaud
This is for the building on Western and Adams
Praise god said the architect
Concrete lines
from man to heaven

The lobby welcomed
When others
Drew a Mason Dixon Line on marble floors

Gather the art
And tell our story
They told Pajaud

Chapter one: a mural
Then sculptures,
then paintings,
then drawings,
then prints

Charles opened the jar of black ink
With it he carved a seat on a rock
Where General Moses could rest
It's a rock on the Indiana bank of the Ohio River

She's looking across the border
She's young
Her gaze takes the speed of light
She's staring at the hills of Tijuana
Past the border patrol helicopters

General Moses sits wearing a white shirt
Then she joins the masses at First and Broadway
Holds a sign
Who's the illegal alien, pilgrim?

Betye's etched bull is a sliced rusted fossil
One leap
From Chavez Ravine
as the dragnet patrol cars pull up
to Florence and Normandie
as the big rig pulls up to the light

The bull leaps from palm tree to palm tree
burning
From bulldozer to bulldozer
Tearing out nopales, calabazas
and roots in South Central

This is for Elizabeth
Your hips are the trunk of the ahuehuete
Your fingers the roots of the caoba
Your branches lower the workers hung by the patrón
Because they didn't cut enough wood

A slab of mahogany in your hands
Becomes love
Two people
Hands melting into shoulders
Cheeks join eyes
Their two wombs form one cradle
Ven aqui
Join us
Abrázanos

Pajaud breaks bread with the artists' spirits
In his garage
The La Brea breeze cools
Carries the smell of Crenshaw, the Nile

Pajaud serves the fish
This time Jonah eats
This time Jonah hears god

The Golden State tribes are dispersed
Pharoah's sold each
To the corners of the earth
Where they dream of their home
on Western and Adams

For Israel Garcia, 2012

This is for Sgt. Israel Garcia
Maricruz's son
The housekeeper

This is for the son of Nayarit

In Cora
Nayarit means
Hijo de dios que está en el cielo y en el sol
Son of god in the heavens and the sun

Israel
A proud Mexican
A proud American
A jackrabbit

His uniform
Decorated
With the bronze star,
the silver star,
the purple heart

This is for the person
Not a Mexicano
Not a Gringo
With a broad smile
Who inspired Steven and company

To go kick some Al Qeda and Taliban ass

Ten years ago
Israel graduated
Four years go he fought in Wanat

The councilwoman
Was at the airport
Heard the mother wail a "come here"
To the casket

The high school cadets
Presented and retrieved
Las banderas
They're not told what things mean
So they go ask soldiers

This is for the widow and others
Who stood
Three days before Memorial Day
And remembered

Now his mother
Lives north of Seattle
The family packs potatoes
The brother
Kills cows

And a plaque
Outside the high school library
Says this Nayarit boy
Is airborne

We My Love

I love the 47 year-old Chicana mothers driving their sanded down '63 Oldsmobiles. I love the 18 year-old Chicano hipsters from Pomona, who have found themselves in Mexico City heavy metal. Heavy nopal. I love the 27 year-old Chicanas who know they have to leave their man, and leave. I love the 35 year-old Chicano single fathers who have come to terms with their mistakes and are raising their sons to love. I love the 7:30 evening barbecues on porches built with so much hope for the future, blind to the eviction notice coming next week. I love the Central American girls who gather under the mural at the golden evening hour, sing praises to God, in hip hop. I love the recien-llegada Armenian girl whose first introduction to American capitalism is, "How many pita with the Tarna chicken?" I love the owners of the Italian deli, in the old neighborhood. They're surrounded by new Mexican homes and metal plating yards. Their past and their future are dictated by the "Italian special." I love the sun when it starts its heavy reclining at twenty to eight, bathing the teporochos with a Midas light. I love Ollin, the neo-indigenist, because le vale madre that we don't really know who the Mexicas really were, their words floating embers toward the sky, their lives cut too short to tell the stories. I love the little restaurant under the freeway over pass, the one with the worst chilaquiles and the most loyal Chicano clients, who come to taste authentic Mexican food. I love the 18 year-old preppy in City Terrace who carries a worn out Bible on Sundays and sits down with Pepe el Tonto to explain why God loves him. "Oh, that's why it rains." "Oh that's why the sun rises." "That's why the hills are green." "That's the answer."

The Words I've Lost

My skin sheds words
A flake falls in Spanish
Two in English

A word falls off my elbow
Off my tongue
Another brushes my earlobe
Bounces off my shoulder
Shatters into
Shell dust
Blows away

They're cradle words
Motherly love words
Father's abandon words

Happens every day

Today at LAX
I lost my mother's first word
Upon birth

Yesterday at Clifton's
ready to pay
I felt around
It was gone
The first word I learned in Spanish

(I still have the second)

Last week, at the roses, in Exposition Park
A word dropped into the fountain
My hand speared to save it
The dot on the "i" plunked and dissolved
It was the word my father whispered,
when he first saw me
whatever it was

In a safe
At the bank
Is my wife's word
After we first held hands

My son scrapes his knees around sentences
I'm loading his arms with words
And he in return gives me some

Segunda Caida

I learned from Lalo Guerrero
that you can cry at 83

He told me of a pretty boy from Tucson
in cowboy boots and hat
who swayed down Main Street, Los Angeles
and stayed to make the city sing

The boy dreamed
of being a ranchera singer

Mexico broke his heart
He forgave
but could not forget
He sang as good as anyone
but when it came to sign the contract
the birth certificate
trumped it all

Now the tears are gone,
the salt clumps into a tombstone

Toltec in the City

For Yreina Cervantez

My other self
you
me
we

strolling
over an LA River bridge,
haters' flayed skin
flapping in the sunset breeze

lying on a bed
of reds and magentas
rollercoastering
on hips
onto my tongue

love me do
as we mouth to mouth
word glyphs

trenzas and cartridges:
cobblestones for freedom

our grandparents' skin:
the color of the smoggy sunset

surface to air
raised fists
take down caravels
bobbing lost
between the clouds

jaguar lips
sink no ships

cyclical hearts
hold babies
soon sacrificed
(on the altar of assimilation)

ride white lilies,
black eagles
along
the gridlocked streets of Nepantla,
Tron-quick turns
to dodge agents' bullets,
deportation cuffs

my wrist,
wrapped by your fingers
as we jump off the bridge
finding tides
for the future

Fires

I asked the poet, do you know anything about Jervey's house?
Salomon posted that his house burned down. Beatriz wrote that it's
like the feeling of losing her house in the war in El Salvador. Hilda
lives close to me in Long Beach. She posted that her relatives's
homes are gone. Cato wrote about the landmarks, loved and gone,
now living as memories: the map maker's home, the Episcopal
Church, the Bunny Museum, the Will Rogers ranch house, the OG
influencer of a century ago.
I told my editor the mission arches in the photo are on the west side
of a courtyard where you drive into the Pasadena Jewish Temple and
Center. You can (yes, I spoke in present tense) park diagonally where
those four and five-foot poles are. Are the flames behind the arches
consuming the homes behind the synagogue? No, I said. That's part
of the Center. The sanctuary is to the right, just outside the yellow
orange photo. It's where I attended services several times last year
on days that I would work late on a Friday and couldn't get down to
Long Beach in time for services. The Rabbi told me staff entered the
buildings and saved 13 Torah scrolls. It was Tuesday. I sat down and
opened the Word file to write the story about the shul. Same feeling
like when I sat down ten years before, to write the obituary of my
spoken word friend, Michele Serros.
On Saturday, Jeff asked me to host in the afternoon. I was on the
air from two in the afternoon to eight at night: updates every ten
minutes, acreage, containment, los muertos, homes called structures,
in the texture of my voice I said memories, displacement, streets,

sidewalks, wood, roofs, laughter, writing, art, ceramics, watercolors, oils, pastels, typewriters.

In L.A. news for almost 25 years and I always thought the Big One was going to be an earthquake.

I'm Just Like You

I'm just like you, I've left everything to come here.
I've buried my grandparents and their words on the hillside.

My parents left me and turned around.
I returned in a coffin to my mother's scream on the runway.

Showers of flowers rained my welcome.

I arrived to work with shovels and spades.
I've had an office with an eagle-god view of the plains.

I sculpted a brass door with a keyhole for every language.

I've looked the powerful straight in the eye and felt helpless.

I've wanted nothing more than a child's arms to cradle me.

I found the love of pressed fingers between bare brick walls.

It was here that my body broke down and withered to smoke.

I conjure the spirit of the forgotten writer,
hold up her notebooks to prove life eternal.

I scored the first goal for the adoring masses.

They light a candle for me each year at services.

My books, sleaze and all, are the talk of the town.

My beloved and I write a present tense story,
each chapter a tasting menu dish paired with the right drink.

I wander the bridges as golden light walks on the river.

We dance bare feet on boards,
while splinters draw blood to write the last words we speak to teach
other.

I've brought God to a people ready to cast it out of rejections.
My algorithm fuels the gas pedal of the symphony sound.

I've stared into eyes behind a red splattered window, a family inside.

I pick, grind, and mix all the right colors
to paint the surge before our arms touch.

I've left this city with love in my arms, doing just fine with what I
remember.

I put the Mason jar under my bed
with grandparents' eyes just before bullets brought end.

I've laid down mint leaves, the big ones; stones on a street.

Yearly, I bring father's wine cup on the day we open the door.

I've put a spoonful of life in my mouth and let it dissolve,
and let vapor come out of my nose
to meet west-bound winds from the desert
that mix with the smoke from the forest flaming within.
It's here I found lips that bloomed the two irises.
I'm just like you, I don't want to leave.

Leaving Los (A Prelude to Fresno)

i.
Goodbye
To the four directions

Goodbye Eastern
Goodbye Western
Goodbye Slauson
Goodbye Ventura

ii.
Before we leave
Let's roll up our pants and wade into the river

Before we leave
Let the river slide its palms under your feet

Before we leave
Let's write our wills on the banks of the river

iii.
It's an open book
Some have written their birth names here
Some have written their death names here
The water will wash the names away

Let's get back in the car
Let's get back on the I-5

Let's wind our way through Burbank

North
Golden

iv.
In spring
the flowers in Gorman
Fill your mouth
Fill your eyes
Fill your ears

v.

As you make your way through the grapevine

Watch out!
Dodge the ghosts of the yellow umbrellas

They're still here
The umbrellas sprint across the freeway
Right there,
a family of yellow umbrellas
Crossing
Father umbrella
holding hand of mother umbrella
holding hand
of daughter umbrella
dangling toward the future

vi.

Slow
Your heartbeat
through the grapevine
Hold tight to the steering wheel

Now
You can see it

There it is in front of you
The San Joaquin Valley

The peach trees sleep
The asparagus shoots
Will one day race for the sun
Not today

vii.

Now
We must decide
Should we take the 5 or the 99
Let's take the 99
To Fresno
Vamos a Fresno

To Fresno

Highway 99 runs

Hear it under the tires
The concrete cracks
My heartbeat

Delano
Then Pixley
McFarland

The grape branches
Arthritic knobs of knuckles
William,
we can't type anymore!

Casi llegamos
A Fresno
El sol es agridulce
En Fresno

In Fulton Mall
Redevelopment
Is sold in fruit cups
Mexicanos walk in Fulton Mall
Hand in hand
With the spirits of those from before
Those who tilled the land
And bought the land

The wind
A five year-old
tumbling, cold giggling
down the Sierras
steep

The wind
Tiptoes Fred Astaire
Across the San Joaquin Valley

Hace frio
En Fresno

The wind chimes
On pesticide faded porches
Hug each other to keep warm

The wind chimes
Are the bones
of the farm workers
at 5:30 in the morning

The dust devil
dances between snoring peach trees
William said, "Use a lasso!"

Ya llegamos
A Fresno

Gaviota

Santa Inés
Mission
Camposanto
Cursive, flowing, bendable
Letters
Headstone

Pedro Pico
Maria Luisa Gonzaga de Ortega
Foster Muñóz

Two miles south of Gaviota beach
the kelp flies
in shallow green

The muddy waters
are below-surface clouds

The gaviotas follow
the coast
they know there's
a mission somewhere south

Waves
thirteen second twins
make
shapes

like earthquake rails
around bends

Windmills

Cartwheel windmills greet
While seven a.m. sun
Scoots us along

The conductor windmill
Sets the pace
Preacher windmill
In early morning faith session
Windmill prayer meeting

Knob jointed oaks
Arthritic oaks
The oaks collect the toll
Like the power lines on the way to Yuma

A prayer meeting we drive by

Raul Salinas pray for us
Marisela Norte pray for us
Alurista pray for us
Señora Enrique pray for us

As we drive the backbone of Califas
From the crumbling schools of 'Sydro
Up cellular gulch

Many Ks of complacency

(if you put your ear to the door you'll hear
"I really want to move to Palo Alto")

The sun glistens off the Bakersfield canals
We navigate the route, careful not to capsize

Water evaporates
Dampens the roots

The fruit basket of the world
Beads on the forehead of
Ignacio, Patricia, Heriberto, Marta, and Gustavo

Fast food is the model of efficiency

Baskets crack
From the dust cropper
A white crust on the handles
And in between her fingernails

Is this
America's finest tourist plantation?

The car was our home and our cell
We got to know each other
"I went to UCLA because Lew Alcindor was there."
"I met the Chicano lawyer over a bottle of Valpolicella."

Inside it turns at its own speed
It flashes by with the speed of history
Talking politics

The old CASA
The old CPUSA

You see, back then everyone was one or the other

The new LIGA
The new English Only
Balanced out by the same old mistakes
Made by new people

The Pacheco Pass
Reservoir
To cherry pit stop

Phone calls to faraway beauty
I want to be close to you...

Bumper to bumper
From here to the Mission

Green bananas
Pupusas
Pisco
The moldy wood of 24th street
The musty corners of the fruit stand

Don't worry we'll be in the bookcases
of Chicano studies one of these days

Jose wrote about the Spine of Califas
We ride the backbone of the state

Travelling from the cancerous tumors of McFarland
To the methyl bromide breeze
in Sherman Heights, Logan Heights

The camera films an empty classroom
"What are we doing here?"
If it could only be so easy for the little ones
If only they could hear, "Yeah Charlie, that's a wrap."

Let's give them back their culture
Let's give them back their language

We crawl the royal highway
In search of the fear that will allow us to see the truth
We visit and revisit the casualties of success

And ahead of us
We'll drive through
The forests of Reies
The boxing ring of Corky
The fields of Jose Angel

Tercera Caida

Yesterday's obituary: a boy from Freedom, PA
Today's obituary: a boy from Apache, OK
Tomorrow's obituary: a Guanajuato boy born el cuatro de julio

Morning

I want to write
when my body is still warm.
When I can still feel the dream, a dream, my dream
evaporating from my skin.
When my skin
still feels freshly peeled from yours.

That moment
of existence, life, consciousness, dream, death, nothingness.
A six-way tug of war
for me.

The warmth escapes,
leaves the womb,
I enter the day.

At that moment,
so many several thoughts remain,
fully formed, ready for me to transcribe.

Then I'm fully awake;
my trusted journal and pen
downstairs.

The cold floor wakes my feet,
my son watches TV, gives me the day's plan.

My wife hugs and breathes me back to the day.
Before I step back into the room
I open the journal on the desk, next to the bookshelf
and the ink flows.

The words come
but they're mostly
packing peanuts.

The warmth of all this
has mostly gone.

And I pray
that I'll have another chance
to do it again.

Ray Say Ta

❧ Swallow first cry, make less lonely ward.

❧ Scrape baptized forehead with Anahuac volcanic rock.

❧ Prick red on dad's embroidered chief.

❧ Knucklehead mom and pops.

❧ Double cross El Norte shopping.

❧ 1978 confuse with Ozhan, both brown.

❧ Learn stories from Jews pool-sunning.

❧ Break glass, not light bulb.

❧ See me sell oranges on the on-ramp.

❧ Get out of dodge rubber bullets.

❧ Tell 5 year-old origins.

❧ Beatbox last breath.

❧ Second line own funeral.

The Treaty

This if for the ones who left
This is for the bicultural scholars
Who became single-minded amnesiacs
This is for the ones who came and moved on
This is for the infant soothsayers
Turned into myopes
By school

A treaty of peace
Friendship
Limits
And settlement
Between the united states of america
and the united mexican states
Without exception of places or persons

Friendship
Limits
And Settlement

In the name of almighty god
animated by a sincere desire
to put an end to the calamities of war
and establish relations of
peace and friendship

benefits upon the citizens of both

Friendship

Limits

And settlement

Without exception of places or persons

Adolfo Guzman-Lopez has been a reporter at LAist 89.3, the National Public Radio affiliate in Los Angeles, since 2000. He's been a poet even longer. In 1994 he co-founded the performance-poetry group The Taco Shop Poets in San Diego. The group toured nationwide for a decade. In the early 2000s he founded the Spine of Califas poetry series with Xiuy Velo and Willie Herron of Los Illegals. But to appreciate how the Mexicano-Chicano-American parts of him were hard to hold together, check out the 1990s Chicano true crime podcast he reported and hosted for LAist Studios, The Forgotten Revolutionary. It won a Golden Mic for 2022. Adolfo lives in Long Beach with his family.

OTHER PROJECTS

Imperfect Paradise: The Forgotten Revolutionary by LAist Studios

An eight episode podcast hosted and reported by Adolfo Guzman-Lopez that investigates the mysterious death of Oscar Gomez, a star of the 1990s Chicano student movement.

Adolfo discovers that the investigation involves coming to terms with painful parts of his own identity as a Chicano, undocumented youth, and a mainstream journalist with an activist past.

You can hear the podcast here or wherever you get your podcasts.

Project 1521

Resistance writing for the 500 years since the fall of the Aztec Empire

Started by Los Angeles-based painter Sandy Rodriguez and Adolfo Guzman-Lopez, Project 1521 gathered 10 poets and artists to reflect on the 500 years since the fall of the Aztec Empire.

The group held workshops, held readings, published a book, and produced a ten-episode podcast. The podcast includes interviews, live recordings, discussions, and original poetry from members of Project 1521. The podcast will give you an insight into the work of modern day Tlacuilos and the publication of their work. You can hear the series through the link below or where your favorite podcasts can be heard.

The Taco Shop Poets

Adolfo Guzman-Lopez co-founded the Taco Shop Poets in 1994. The group produced CDs (Chorizo Tonguefire, Intersection), and published "Anthology: Chorizo Tonguefire." Introduction by George Lipsitz. Edited by Adrian Arancibia and Stephanie De La Torre. The group toured across the country for about a decade and was featured in documentaries including Americanos: Latino Life in the United States.

HINCHAS Press

HINCHAS Press is a Los Angeles-based micropress that publishes zines, poetry, poetry in translation, and library science non-fiction. HINCHAS supports social justice initiatives, and advocates for bilingual literacy endeavors, especially along portions of the Américas that are monolingual.

HINCHAS Press seeks to showcase the fiction, poetry, and prose of authors from las América and America. In terms of taste and content, we firmly believe the content to be the medium. To that end, we seek to publish innovative, experimental work of a devastating caliber, regardless of format, dialect, or pedigree.

www.ingramcontent.com/pod-product-compliance
Lightning Source LLC
Chambersburg PA
CBHW051205120626
46547CB00013B/1207